GH00383633

Acknowledgements

This text replaces *Crouch End – A Walk* by Bridget Cherry and Ken Gay published in 1995 but in compiling the new text, constant reference has been made to the original.

With thanks to Lesley Ramm, who walked with me, Janet Owen and the Hornsey Historical Society Publications Committee and Archive. The photographs are by Lesley Ramm and Eleri Rowlands unless otherwise credited and the map by Peter Garland.

Introduction

Crouch End is situated in a valley at the eastern end of the Northern Heights of London, at the meeting place of several ancient routes. It is probably so named after a cross sited at the junction of these routes and the name first appears in records in 1465 as Crouche End.

A small medieval settlement grew up at this meeting place, by the boundary of Topsfield Manor within the Parish of Hornsey. The old routes still exist, with one coming from Islington over Crouch Hill and the other from Holloway over Crouch End Hill. After meeting at Crouch End Broadway they divide, with one going north along Park Road following the old pilgrim route to the holy well in Muswell Hill and the other going along Tottenham Lane to the parish church in Hornsey High Street and then onwards to Tottenham. In the early nineteenth century the settlement was still a cluster of small cottages at the foot of Crouch End Hill with larger houses in their own grounds around what is now The Broadway.

Change began with the construction of the Great Northern Railway and the opening of Hornsey Station in 1850, but the main impetus came with the opening of stations on Crouch Hill and Crouch End Hill in 1867-8. Old estates were sold to developers with a resulting massive increase in population between 1870 and 1900. By 1890 the late Victorian shopping centre we now see had become the main centre of Hornsey eclipsing the old village by the parish church.

On your walks around the area, we will attempt to illustrate how the transformation from rural hamlet to London suburb was achieved.

Transport

W7 bus runs from Wells Terrace, Finsbury Park Station through Crouch End Broadway to Muswell Hill Broadway

W5 bus runs from Archway Underground Station through The Broadway to the Arena Shopping Centre, Green Lanes, Harringay

41 bus runs from Archway Underground Station through The Broadway, past Turnpike Lane Underground Station to Tottenham Hale Station

91 bus runs from Trafalgar Square through The Broadway and terminates by the YMCA in Tottenham Lane

W3 bus runs From Wells Terrace, Finsbury Park Station, across Tottenham Lane at Ferme Park Road and on to Northumberland Par

London Overground serves Crouch Hill Station

National Rail from Moorgate serves Hornsey and Harringay Statior

Walks

The area has been divided into four short self contained walk beginning and ending at The Broadway, but these can be easily linke to form a longer walk.

Clock Tower 1895

WALK ONE
Clock Tower to Park Road

Two buildings dominate Crouch End and the first two walks begin at one of these, the **Clock Tower** (1) which was designed by F G Knight and built in 1894-5 as a testimonial to Henry Reader Williams (1822-97). He was the chairman of the Local Board and for twenty years steered Hornsey through the rapid change from village to suburb. Williams worked tirelessly to preserve Hornsey's open spaces and was especially prominent in the campaign to save Highgate Woods. The tower has a handsome granite base which is surmounted by stripes of red and yellow Mansfield stone. The upper part of red brick is crowned by a terracotta cupola. On the side facing The Broadway is a portrait medallion of Williams designed by his friend Sir Alfred Gilbert (creator of Eros in Piccadilly).

Clock Tower medallion

Behind the Clock Tower is **Topsfield Parade** (2) which is built in the angle between Middle Lane and Tottenham Lane on what was originally the site of Topsfield Hall, a Georgian house, the home of Henry Weston Elder. Elder died in 1882 and after the death of his widow Sarah, in 1892, part of the estate was sold to builders

Topsfield Parade

3

Topsfield Hall 1894 (NMPS *Collection HHS Arch*

Edmondson & Son of Highbury. The Hall was demolished in 18
and James Edmondson built the four storied curved parade, wi
a multiplicity of gables and windows of a different design on eve
floor, along the Hall's old boundary.

No 2 Park Road

Keep to the left of the Clo
Tower and turn into Park Roa
formerly known as Mayna
Street, which leads to Musw
Hill. This is an older pocket
development which was bu
when Topsfield Hall was st
standing. **No. 2 Park Roa**
(3) at the corner with Midd
Lane is now the Monkey Nu
steak house but from 1852 wa

Boden Bros, corn chandlers with a post office at the rear. Furth
down on the left on the corner with Wolseley Road stands the **forme
woodwork building** (4) of Crouch End Schools. It was built in 18
by H. Chatfeild Clarke as a
addition to the main scho
buildings of 1877 in Wolsele
Road. These buildings late
became the Lower School o
Highgate Wood School, whic
is in Montenotte Road on th
edge of Crouch End Playin
Fields. Crouch End School wa
demolished, to be replaced i
1994, by Topsfield Close. Th
building on Park Road with it
battlemented corner turre
was converted in 1990 int
residential accommodatio

59 Park Road former woodwork building

Crouch End Schools stone

with shops in the formerly open arcade below. The end shop No. 59C, Change of Heart, has the **original name stone** (4) of Crouch End Schools 1877 (now broken into three pieces) which was rescued from the demolition by a previous owner.

Continuing towards Muswell Hill, **Park Road Leisure Centre** (5) is based on the former Borough of Hornsey Open Air Swimming Pool established in 1929. It is now refurbished with a large indoor pool, diving pool and training pool, as well as the outdoor pool. Just before the Leisure Centre, at No. 145 is

Abide Church window

Abide Church (6). Built in the late 1920s as Park Road Gospel Hall, its present congregation, part of the Ichthus Christian Fellowship, continues the evangelical tradition and now shares its premises

Health Centre and War Memorial

with the Tamil language Grace Church. On the other side of the Leisure Centre is Fuller Court built on the site of the nurses' home of the former Hornsey Central Hospital. The hospital itself, which was built by public subscription in 1910, was demolished in 2007 and

Hornsey War Memorial

Crouch End Playing Fields

replaced by a **Health Centre** (7). This backs on to **Crouch End Playing Fields** (8) which were established in 1890 and which remain the home of several cricket and tennis clubs having been preserved from redevelopment by local residents. The only remaining part of the hospital is the **War Memorial** (7), opened in 1921, which houses oak boards bearing the names of nearly 1300 Hornsey men who died in the First World War. The Memorial, which is now a listed building, can be accessed from inside the health centre during the centre's opening hours.

War Memorial Board 38

Ramsey Court Park Road

Across the road from the health centre is **Ramsey Court** (9), the largest block of flats in Crouch End. These were built by Hornsey Council in 1952 on a site devastated by a V1 bomb in October 1944. The old Hornsey Borough Council was very active in the provision of social housing and **Kelland Close** (10), along Park Road towards Crouch End, was the last of their slum clearance schemes to be built in 1938 before the onset of the Second World War. Yet further towards Crouch End are two pubs. There has been a pub called the Princess Alexandra on the site of **The Alex** (11), re-opened under that name at the beginning of 2015, for over one hundred years. The original building was destroyed by bombing in the Second World War and rebuilt in 1952. For a short period it was named Villiers Terrace. On the corner with Lynton Road is **The Maynard Arms** (12) (formerly The Maynard and the Hungry Horse) which was built in 1851. It commemorates Park Road's previous name of Maynard Street, after a medieval Lord of the Manor.

Maynard Arms

Mission Hall, The Grove

Keystone New Road

13 **14** **15** In the triangle between Middle Lane and Park Road lie Lynto Road and The Grove, at the end of which is the John Farrer (184 1930) designed 1881 **Mission Hall** (13) now converted to housin as No. 49. Part of the same 1850 development is **New Road** (1. The terraced houses on the right hand side (entering from Pa Road) have unusual brick details and the ground floor doors an windows have curiously elongated keystones. Further down on th right is **Back Lane** (15); the charming little Topsfield Cottages we rescued from squalor and refurbished in the early 1970s.

Proceed from New Road into Middle Lane and turn right, passin Nos. 9 – 35 an engaging terrace of pairs of cottages. Look across th road to the fading painted notice for Westerns Laundry on the wa at the corner of Middle Lane Mews with the end of Topsfield Parad Return to the Clock Tower.

Westerns Laundry Middle Lane Mews

Back Lane sign

Back Lane Cottages

Weston Park Road

Western Park to Tottenham Lane

Weston Park (16), to the right of the Clock Tower, was developed on part of the Elder estate by the architect John Farrer. Building began in 1885 and by 1900, Farrer had designed 93 houses for this road. The houses are large semi detached properties, many with the then fashionable Dutch gables and some, such as the two on either corner with **Felix Avenue** (17), with striking turrets. The names of Weston Park and of Elder Avenue further down on the left, commemorate the last owner of the Topsfield Estate. On No. 13 is an unofficial blue plaque to the silent movie actress Lilian Harvey who was born there in 1906. On the right hand side also is an entrance leading to a former health clinic and the rear of Hornsey Town Hall. This substantial area between Haringey Park and Weston Park awaits redevelopment, associated with the future plans for the Town Hall.

Corner of Weston Park & Felix Avenue

It is well worth walking further along Weston Park simply to enjoy the variety of house design but also to see **Union Church** (18) on the corner of Weston Park and Ferme Park Road. Union Church was formed by the union of the Congregationalists in Park Chapel and the Baptists in Ferme Park Church in 1974. The

Ferme Park Baptist Church (HHS Archive)

(19) modern church and community centre are the third on the site and opened in 1980, replacing the magnificent 1900 Baptist Church with a corner turret which was demolished in 1973.

Union Church

Return to Elder Avenue and walk past its attractive houses towards Tottenham Lane, passing on the left hand side **Earl Haig Hall** (19). This building with its distinctive stepped facade, was opened in 1928 as a British Legion Hall, its name honouring the former Commander in Chief of the British Army in France during the First World War, who died that year. It has functioned since 2013 as a community-

Earl Haig Hall

focused pub, right next door to Crouch End's grandest public house The Queens.

The Queens stained glass

The Queens entrance

The Queens interior

The Queens (20) on the corner with Tottenham Lane and at the end of Broadway Parade, is a splendid example of a Victorian gin palace built in 1899 by John Cathles Hill (1858 -1915). Its stately entrance with columns and arches encased in granite and terracotta, leads to an interior which survives largely intact, with decorative plasterwork ceilings and glazed mahogany bar partitions. The superb Art Nouveau glass was made by the local firm Cakebread Robey. Although now solely a gastro pub, it was opened as a hotel and still has the original name on the side elevation and on the floors of the entrances.

Turn right into Tottenham Lane and walk past the former Deco offices of the *Hornsey Journal* to the **Arthouse** (21). This building, now a cinema, the first to open in Crouch End for many years, began life in 1912 as a Salvation Army Citadel. The most recent renovation of the building has once again exposed on its frontage the four foundation stones which had been painted over by previous occupants. Across the road is the **YMCA hostel** (22) which has developed on this site since its

Arthouse

opening in 1929 and which was extensively remodelled in the 1990s.

Continue on this side of Tottenham Lane back towards The Broadway. Nos. 46 and 46A show the original shop fronts for 'Margaretta, Dressmaker' and 'Rickard, Shoe Repairs' although the shop itself is a deli! Look up as you cross Elder Avenue, and at roof level is a

Hornsey YMCA

Old Shop Fronts 46 Tottenham Lane

(23) date stone 1895 recording when Topsfield Parade was built. The health club at No. **31 Topsfield Parade** (23) has a large lunette window on the facade reflecting the original facade of the Queen's Opera House, a theatre seating 1200 people. Subsequently known as Crouch End Hippodrome, it initially hosted West End productions, but eventually

1895 date stone Topsfield Parade

became a music hall and finally a cinema although it continued to stage the occasional live performance up to the Second World War. The original building was destroyed by fire in 1942 and rebuilt in 1958 by the mail order firm Gratton Ltd. It remained in their possession until in 2006 it became the Virgin Active Health Centre.

Health Club 31 Topsfield Parade

The parade of shops opposite Topsfield Parade, from the corner of Elder Avenue to the corner of Weston Park is known as **Broadway Parade** (24) and was constructed by John Cathles Hill, but the attractive building at the end of the parade, with a square turret, was designed by John Farrer for H Williams & Co. as The Creamery; the cows walking along Tottenham Lane for milking in the days when Crouch End was still a rural hamlet. After many years as a restaurant, it is now a bakery/

Gail's Bakery - The Creamery

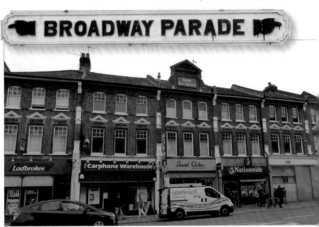

Bank Buildings The Broadway

patisserie. The building on the opposite corner of Weston Park started life as a branch of the London and South Western Bank and 'Established 1862' on the pediment refers to the establishment date of the bank not of the construction of this building. Subsequently a branch of Barclays Bank and a KFC food outlet, it awaits a new role. This building is one corner of the John Farrer designed **Bank Buildings** (25) one of the first parades of shops to appear in Crouch End after the coming of the railway and with its name displayed in the centre above the top storey. After passing Bank Buildings the other iconic building in Crouch End is reached. The Town Hall is the start of our remaining two walks.

The old bank building 1862

13

Hornsey Town Hall

WALK THREE
The Town Hall to Crouch Hil

26 In the 1920s the tiny Council offices of the Borough of Hornsey wer in Southwood Lane, Highgate, and were totally inadequate for th functioning of the borough. At that point the Council bought two plot of land (which originally formed part of the garden of Old Crouch Hal fronting on to Crouch End Broadway. These were laid out as a publ park and were eventually selected as the site for the new town ha A competition for the best design was launched in 1933 and the firs prize from 218 entries went to a New Zealander, Reginald Harold Ure (1906-1988). The resulting **Hornsey Town Hall** (26) is an asymmetric building with the public hall to the left distinguished by the elongate windows of the foyer above a generous triple entrance. The Counc offices are entered under the tower by a smaller but more decorativ entrance with a stone lintel by the sculptor Arthur J Ayres (1902-198 and ornamental metalwork. The Council chamber is reached internall by a fine staircase of Ashburton marble. Hornsey Town Hall wa

Hornsey Town Hall fountain and forecourt

14

Hornsey Town Hall square

Hornsey Town Hall entrance door

Hornsey Town Hall porch detail

Gas Showrooms Uren plaque

awarded the bronze medal of the Royal Institute of British Architects for the best London building built between 1933 and 1935 and the plaque for this award can be seen to the left of the Council office entrance.

Hornsey Town Hall RIBA medal

27 The forecourt of the Town Hall was formerly the site of Broadway Hall which burned down in 1923 and which had housed a succession of different religious denominations. For a short time in the mid nineteenth century it was the meeting place of the Highways Board, a forerunner of the Local Board, an interesting link with the later Town Hall. In 1935 the Hornsey Gas Company purchased Nos. and 10 Crouch End Broadway and built their showrooms on the south side of the forecourt.

Barclays Bank entrance

Designed by Dawe and Carter, this building featured a new type of curved window popular at the time (also used for Heals on Tottenham Court Road) and included on the first floor a demonstration theatre. The exterior was decorated below the first floor window with stone panels by Arthur Ayres, carved in low relief and depicting scenes relating to the gas industry. Although this **former gas showroom** (27) now houses a branch of Barclays Bank, it still retains all its original features including the windows and the carved panels.

28 To complete the complex of buildings, the site of the Mountview Telephone Exchange alongside the new Town Hall was due to become vacant with the building of a new telephone exchange on Crouch End Hill and so in 1937 the Electricity Supply Company (electricity supply was a borough undertaking) purchased No. 26 The Broadway to build a showroom on the site, at the same time converting the old exchange to offices. This building, also designed by Uren, is simpler and was completed in 1939, with its chief decorative feature a carved brick relief of the Spirit of Electricity, again by Ayres, placed high above the office entrance. The **former electricity showroom** (28) is now a popular restaurant with tables on the north side of the Town Hall forecourt.

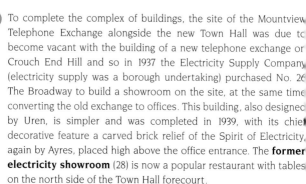

Walk round the forecourt, noticing the splendid chestnut trees planted to commemorate the silver wedding of King George VI and Queen Elizabeth. Enter Hatherley Gardens and walk to the **fountain** (29) which is on the end wall of Hornsey Library. Set in a pool with a curtain of water jets is a bronze sculpture of a reclining woman by T B Huxley-Jones, FRBS (1908-1968). On the back wall of the fountain are two small plaques, one an outline shape of the old Borough of Hornsey (1903-1965) with the borough motto and the other of Hornsey's medieval church tower.

Spirit of Electricity by Ayres

Hornsey Library (30) in Haringey Park was opened in 1965 just before the demise of the old Hornsey Borough. Designed by the Borough's Architectural Design Department, it is a three storey building with a projecting porch under which is a stone unveiled by Princess Alexandra at its opening. An interesting feature of the interior of the library is an engraved glass window on the staircase showing the historical buildings of Hornsey. This was designed by Frederick J Mitchell, ARCA (1903-1982) former head of art at Hornsey School of Art.

Hornsey Library fountain

Floral Hall

31 **32** **33** **34** In 1845, **Haringey Park** (31) was the first road to be laid out i Crouch End since medieval times. By 1871 this private, gated roa contained 25 solid middle class residences, a few of which surviv today, although in many cases, their rear gardens have been take up with more modern housing. Turn right from the library toward Crouch Hill noting the interesting **Floral Hall** (32) which was adde on the corner in 1929 as a greengrocer and florist. **Nos. 118 and 12**

(33) Crouch Hill were probably built in the 1820s, (though No. 120 may date back to 1790) and are attractive, low built Regency houses. **Abbotts Terrace** (34) the narrow lane running between No. 118 and the backs of the houses in Cecile Park is a still older relic, as it appears as a separate strip of land on the 1815 Hornsey Enclosure map.

Abbots Terrace cottages

35 **Kestrel House** (formerly Cecile House) (35) on the corner with Cecile Park at No. 104 is a substantial mansion of c. 1870. Now a school for autistic children, it was the home of the Mountview Theatre Schoo from 1945. On its facade is a Haringey green plaque

commemorating the amateur photographer George Shadbolt who recorded the area in rural times and who lived here from 1865 Next to the school is Ivor Court, a block of flats which in 1960 replaced Durham House. In June 1916 the Hornsey Auxiliary Military Hospital opened here in a former school and by the time it closed at the end of the war it had

Kestrel House

130 beds. The original house called Amedee Villa probably looked very like Cecile House. The upper slopes of Crouch Hill were already known by the mid eighteenth century as Mount Pleasant and by the early nineteenth century the area was scattered with wealthy country villas and mansions including Womersley House the home of Mr Peter Robinson of the Oxford Street department store. The only survivor of such houses is the remnant of Crouch Hill House now embedded in **St Gildas RC Junior School** (36) in Dickenson Road.

It is worth stopping at the top of the hill to take in the spectacular views. To the south are the different shapes of the City skyscrapers and to the north Alexandra Palace dominates the horizon. Although this part is in the London Borough of Islington note the **Parkland Walk** (37) which opened in 1984, running below the road. It follows the

Parkland Walk Crouch End Station platforms

route of the Edgware, Highgate and London Railway constructed in 1867 and which ran from Finsbury Park to Alexandra Palace. The onset of the Second World War delayed its planned electrification and incorporation into the Northern Line. After the war, the plans were abandoned and the line was closed to passengers in 1954. It is now a 4.5 km long green pathway through the otherwise dense urban environment in which muntjac deer are occasionally seen.

Islington and Hornsey parish boundary s

Cross to the left side of the road (facing north to Alexandra Palac and note the pathway signed **Vicarage Path** (38), one of sever paths in this area which predate the coming of the railway. Vicarag Path emerges in Haslemere Road. At the kerb edge near here is worn upright stone, the remains of the 1741 **boundary marker** (3 between Hornsey and Islington parishes. The present day marke is a metal sign on the other side of the road, welcoming you to th London Borough of Haringey – Crouch End.

Crouch Hill Red Gables (HHS Archive

40 Further down the hill on the left is Haslemere Road. It and the nearb Christchurch and Waverley Roads which run between Crouch Hill an Crouch End Hill were all developed during the 1880s on the estate c Oakfield House. Many of the late Victorian houses and some simila in Crouch Hill were built around 1891 by W J Collins (1856-1936) th builder responsible for the development of much of Muswell Hill At No. 113 Crouch Hill, on the corner with Haslemere Road is **Re**

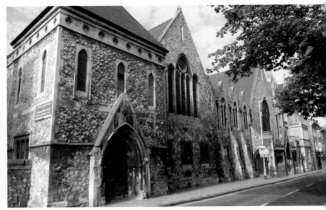

Park Chapel Crouch Hill

Gables (40) which has an abundance of the picturesque motifs architects such as Norman Shaw made popular in the 1870s – tall chimneys, terracotta plaques and elaborate gables.

Approaching the bottom of the hill, the former Congregational **Park Chapel** (41) is the dominant building. Started in 1854-5 by a congregation which had begun by meeting in a house in Park Road, the original chapel consisted of the central gable of the present chapel, which looks down Haringey Park. The congregation increased rapidly under the Rev John Corbin and Rev Dr Alfred Rowland, making frequent enlargements necessary. By 1866 the enlarged church could hold 1480 people. After the advent of the Crouch End Board Schools in 1877 the church schoolroom was no longer needed and was replaced by the Corbin Memorial Hall in 1893. The foundation stone laid by Dr Alfred Rowland in September 1892 can be seen on the exterior. The union of the Park Chapel congregation with the Baptists

in Ferme Park Road in 1974 meant that the chapel became redundant. Since then the buildings have been used for a variety of purposes. Currently the chapel is used for worship by the Eternal Sacred Order of Cherubim and Seraphim and is known as Mount Zion Cathedral. This church was founded in 1925 and was born out of the Anglican Church community among the Yoruba people of Western Nigeria. The

Park Chapel interior

Corbin Hall is used for various recording activities.

Walk past Park Chapel and the nearby Harringay Arms back to The Broadway and the end of the third walk.

Dunn's Bakery

The Broadway to Crouch End Hill

(42) The fourth and final walk also begins in The Broadway. Before crossing the road at the foot of Crouch Hill look up. Above No. 6, **Dunn's Bakery**, (42) is a wheat sheaf bearing the date 1850 and the initials W M. In 1850 William Muddiman ran the post office and bakers here, across the road from Batterby's forge which stood, before its demolition in 1895, where the National Westminster Bank is now, in the angle between Crouch Hill and Crouch End Hill. Take the right side and walk up

WM 1850 above Dunn's

(43) Crouch End Hill past the 1930s half timbered **Railway Tavern** (4. and on past the 1937 brick **Mountview Telephone Exchange** (43

Batterby's Forge (NMPS *Collection HHS Archive*

22

This was built on the site of Oakfield Villa and was Crouch End's first really large building.

Further up the hill on the left are Christchurch and Waverley Roads. Hornsey School of Art was established in Waverley Road in 1882 by Charles Swinstead (1815-1890) as a private art school. Subsequently taken over by Middlesex County Council in 1920, it was extended in 1931 and renamed the Hornsey College of Arts and Crafts. Although the Fine Arts Department moved to Alexandra Palace in 1965, it became known for a series of student sit-ins starting

in May 1968. The college moved from here in 1981. Opposite, where Waverley Road joins Haslemere Road, next to No. 4, lies the other end of Vicarage Path, marked by an attractive **Victorian signpost** (44). No. 10 bears an English Heritage blue plaque (45) commemorating **Frank Matcham** (1854-

Fingerpost in Haslemere Road

1920) the well known theatre architect and designer, who lived in the house between 1895 and 1904. The kink in Haslemere Road allowed for the drive to Oakfield House which survived as a private boys' preparatory school until 1933. After demolition it was replaced by the present Oakfield Court flats.

Return to Crouch End Hill and turn right to view what is now part of **Coleridge Primary School** (46). The central building in classical style was built in 1931 for the Hornsey School of Art and was retained when the building was taken over in 1984 by the Trades Union Congress National Education Centre, then acquired in 2008 to be remodelled

as an extension for Coleridge School. Continue to the top of the hill to the shops; they are all that remains of Crouch End Hill Station, which was opened in August 1867. The bridge over the railway has been remodelled with a parapet of inverted arches and it is possible to look over to the platforms of the old station and to access the Parkland Walk here.

Coleridge Primary School

Crescent Road green

47 Cross the road, noting the original, sixties-style, Coleridge Primary School set back from the carriageway and turn into **Crescent Road** (47). It was laid out in the 1870s in an irregular curve around Christ Church with substantial detached Gothic houses of which nine survive. Behind the triangle with trees, at the junction with Avenue

No 1 Avenue Road

Road, fragments of the tenth remain at No. 1 Avenue Road. These fragments have been incorporated into a garden terrace in front of old people's flats. Crescent Road continues its curve and rejoin Crouch End Hill below the church with the modern church hall on the site of the original vicarage on the right.

48 **Christ Church** (48) sits back from the road in an attractive leafy churchyard. It was begun in 1861 as the new parish church for Crouch End, the congregation having previously been worshipping in the old Broadway Hall. The land, formerly part of the Crouch Hall estate, was given by the developer Charles Scrase Dickins, his only stipulation being that no school should be built on the land. The church, in traditional Gothic style, is an

Christ Church

early work by Arthur Blomfield (1822-1899) and began modestly. However an increasing congregation led to the addition of a south aisle in 1867, a tower and spire in 1873 and a porch in 1883. The building committee insisted that it be built in Kentish ragstone in contrast with the brick Blomfield had used in nearby Holy Innocents Church, Tottenham Lane. The carved capitals in the interior of the church were paid for by members of the congregation and one bears the name of its donor while another has rope depicted in the design, its donor being a naval officer.

Christ Church Nave & Chancel

The church hall in Crescent Road was built to replace a Sunday School hall the church had built in 1878 in nearby newly developed Edison Road,

Christ Church William Block capital

which apart from housing the Sunday School also had facilities for concerts, lectures and a library. Decreased use and increasing maintenance costs meant that the hall was finally sold by the church in 1998. Turn left into **Edison Road** (49) and the hall is still there on the right hand side, as the Shahmaghsoudi School of Islamic Sufism. Opposite the hall are the attractively painted earliest houses in the road with gables and fancy bargeboards and further down from it on the same side are the Church Cottages, courtyard and a tucked

Edison Road Halls

away doctor's surgery. Walk down the road to Coleridge Road. In 1882 twelve roads were laid out in the grounds of the former Crouch Hall, by the Imperial Property Development Co., between Coolhurst Road and Park Road. In Wolseley, Coleridge, Coolhurst and Crouch Hall Roads two storeyed Queen Anne style houses were built. It is worth wandering up the road to view some of the details of these houses or turn right into Coleridge Road and walk to its junction with The Broadway. On this corner is the **Kings Head** (50) public house. It is dated 1887 and has a fat corner turret. This building replaced an inn of the same name further up Crouch End Hill which had records going back to the seventeenth century.

Church Cottages courtyard Edison Road

To the left, on the site from Budgens to the corner with Crou[ch] Hall Road, is a parade of shops which was once the location of J[ames] Wilson, Crouch End's own department store which its owner Jam[es] Wilson in 1906 described as a 'rendezvous of the elite'. Wilson w[as] an enlightened employer who provided pleasant accommodati[on] for his employees and was one of the first traders to introduce a[n] early closing day. Sadly Wilsons closed in 1971 and the old store w[as] demolished to be replaced by the buildings there today. So the four[?] walk ends, back in the centre of Crouch End's shopping area.

King's Head PH

Bibliography

Most of these books are available from the Hornsey Historical Society in the Old School House, 136 Tottenham Lane, N8 7EL.
More information from **www.hornseyhistorical.org.uk**.

150 Years of Christ Church 1862 – 2012
by Sheila Wheeler, 2012

The Book of Crouch End
by Ben Travers, Barracuda Books Ltd, 1990

Civic Pride in Hornsey The Town Hall and its surrounding buildings
by Bridget Cherry, HHS, revised 2006

Crouch End Clock Tower
by Joan Schwitzer, HHS, 1995

Gin and Hell-fire
Compiled and edited by Peter Barber, HHS, 2004

Hornsey and Crouch End
by Ken Gay, Chalford Publishing Co., 1998

Hornsey Past Crouch End Muswell Hill Hornsey
by Steven Denford, Historical Publications Ltd., 2008

John Farrer The Man who changed Hornsey
by Janet Owen, HHS, 2009

A Vision of Middlesex
by Janet Owen & John Hinshelwood, HHS, 2011

BARRINGTON
9
HAREFIELD RD.
CARYSFORT
RD.
RD.
7
5
6
Playing
Fields
8
10
PALACE
11
13
THE GROVE
PARK
TIVOLI RD.
RD
RD
GLASSLYN
4
R
MONTENOTTE
RD.
WOLSELEY
RD.
BERKELEY
SHANKLIN RD.
RUSSELL RD.
BEDFORD
RD.
BIRCHINGTON
CLIFTON
COOLHURST
HALL
CROUCH
ROAD
RD.
HURST
AV.
COLERIDGE
Sports
Field
COURTSIDE
ROAD
CRESCENT
RD
48
47
47
AVENUE
ROAD
CRESCENT RD
Walk
Parkland
CROUCH
HORNSEY LANE